Copyright Page
MVP's Playbook

MVP'S PLAYBOOK

TRADARA MCLAURINE

GASPAR SABATER

Dedication

To my children, thank you for your strength, your resilience, your love and your joy. You helped me bounce back in more ways than you'll ever know. Remember, whenever you feel as if you have no one to talk to, you can always talk to Him.

TABLE OF CONTENTS

CHAPTER 1
THE STAR PLAYER

CHAPTER 2
THE INJURY

CHAPTER 3
THE BENCH

CHAPTER 4
TRYOUTS

CHAPTER 5
MICAH

CHAPTER 6
P.A.S.S. IT TO ME

CHAPTER 7
MVP

Opening quote

"Trust in the Lord with all your heart and lean not on your own understanding; in all your ways submit to him, and he will make your paths straight." — *Proverbs 3:5–6*

"It's not whether you get knocked down, it's whether you get back up." — Vince Lombardi

CHAPTER 1:
THE STAR PLAYER

Micah Virgil Phillips, best known as MVP, woke at 5:30 AM sharp, to the sound of bouncing basketballs—a fitting start to his day. Just as he'd done every other day for the past several years, he hopped out of bed, threw on his workout clothes, laced up his sneakers, and headed out to the driveway where his personal basketball hoop stood waiting. The air was crisp, but the cold didn't bother him. This was his time to put in extra work before school.

His morning drill went the same as always: a hundred free throws, fifty layups from each side, and dribbling exercises that tested his control and speed. He envisioned himself in high-stakes games, counting down the final seconds before sinking the winning shot. His heart pounded as he imagined the crowd chanting his name. MVP! MVP!

After his workout, he rushed inside to shower, grab a granola bar, and headed out the door with his bookbag over one shoulder and his basketball tucked under his arm.

MVP enjoyed school. Math was his favorite subject, but when Mrs. Christian started to teach on how to find the volume of various shapes and drew the sphere on the white board MVP thought the sphere looked like a basketball, and he forgot all about paying attention to his math teacher. He drifted off into a daydream about being a great basketball star.

At lunch MVP hurried to the gym to hang out with his teammates. They loved discussing game strategy and sharing highlights from the NBA. His friends were great—the best part of playing basketball besides winning, of course.

MVP knew winning was wonderful because, with his help, his team won a lot. He wasn't just a good player; he was the player. The one everyone looked up to, the one expected to lead the team to victory.

Practice after school was intense, but MVP thrived under pressure. His coach pushed the team hard, and MVP pushed himself even harder. Every drill, every scrimmage, every critique—he absorbed it all, always striving to be better. The sound of sneakers squeaking against the floor, the rhythmic pounding of the ball, the sharp whistle of the coach—all of it was music to his ears.

After practice ended, MVP took the long way home, as he always did, making a detour past the park where kids from all over the neighborhood played pickup games. He loved watching them, seeing the raw talent and love for the game.

A younger kid named Beckham came running up to him, tugging on his bookbag. "MVP! MVP! Can you show me that move you did at the game last Saturday? The one where you turn in a circle before dunking!"

MVP smiled, always willing to share his love for the game. "Sure, little man," he said, walking towards the court. He set his bookbag down, took off his jacket, and grabbed the ball.

He started dribbling down the court, bouncing the ball under his right leg, then under his left. With a powerful leap, he soared into the air. The kids at the park watched with big, bright eyes and wide-open mouths. MVP spun midair, preparing to dunk. But as he came down, something went wrong. His right foot landed awkwardly, and a sharp pain shot through his knee. He crumpled to the ground, clutching his leg and screaming in pain.

CHAPTER 2:
THE INJURY

Pain surged through MVP's knee like a lightning bolt—sharp and persistent. The happy sounds of the park—kids laughing, basketballs smacking the blacktop, sneakers squeaking—faded into a dull hum as he lay on the ground, clutching his leg. His breaths were short, his mind reeling with panic. This wasn't just a dislocation. This felt different.

Beckham stood frozen for a second before yelling for help. Within moments, a crowd gathered around him, murmuring in concern. An onlooker dialed 911, and soon, the distant sound of sirens cut through the evening air.

The paramedics worked swiftly, stabilizing his leg and loading him onto the stretcher. The flashing red and blue lights blurred as MVP stared up at the sky, his heart pounding in his ears. He had never felt so helpless.

The ride to the hospital felt endless. MVP clenched his fists, his mind racing. What if it was really bad? What if he couldn't play anymore? Basketball wasn't just a game—it was his life. The thought of losing it sent a wave of fear through him.

His parents arrived at the hospital at the same time as the ambulance. His mother bent over the gurney, brushing his forehead. "We're here, baby. We're here." His father stood on the other side, his strong hand squeezing MVP's shoulder. "Hang in there, son."

At the hospital, the doctor examined him carefully and ordered X-rays. The waiting was unbearable. MVP's knee throbbed, but the worst pain was in his chest—it came from not knowing if he'd ever play basketball again.

Finally, the doctor returned, holding a clipboard. He sighed before speaking to the family. "You've torn your ACL," the doctor said, his tone serious but calm. "It's an important tissue that helps keep your knee stable. We can fix it with surgery, but you'll need to rest your knee for at least six months."

"SIX MONTHS!?" MVP said louder than he intended. His stomach dropped. "Six months!? I'll miss the entire season!"

His mother gave him a sympathetic look and squeezed his hand. His father leaned in, placing a steady hand on his shoulder. "Son," he whispered, "P.A.S.S. it to me." The words barely registered. All MVP could hear was the echo of his dreams slipping further and further away. He had spent years preparing for his freshman varsity debut. Now, in a single moment, it was gone. MVP's world felt shattered. The court, the one place where he felt unstoppable had been ripped away from him. And he had no idea how to get it back.

CHAPTER 3:
THE BENCH

After the surgery, when MVP went back to school, everyone was kind. His classmates and teammates said things like, "You'll be back to 100% in no time," or "Don't worry, bro. This is just a little set back," and his coach assured him that he was still a very important part of the team.

But sitting on the bench was nothing like playing. Game after game, practice after practice, MVP watched from the sidelines as his team carried on without him.

At first, he tried to stay positive. He cheered for his teammates, encouraged them, and studied their plays. He told himself this was temporary, that he'd be back soon. But as time passed, frustration and sadness grew. The fire that had fueled him on the court was dimming. He wanted to be out there, making plays, leading his team. Not stuck on the sidelines feeling useless. Watching wasn't enough.

One afternoon during practice, as he sat watching yet another scrimmage, something inside him snapped. He gritted his teeth and grabbed his crutches. He couldn't just sit there anymore.

He stood up abruptly, his knee aching in protest. The team barely noticed as he walked out of the gym, the weight of his injury pressing down on him harder than ever. This time, he didn't take the long way home past the park. He didn't even want to look at a basketball.

When he arrived home, his dad greeted him at the door. "Hey, Son."

"Hey, Dad," MVP replied quietly with his head down walking toward his room.

His father watched him for a moment, then said, "Son, remember: P.A.S.S. it to me."

He turned to his father. "What if I don't want to just sit on the bench?"

His father smiled. "Then don't."

That night, MVP made a decision. He was going to fight. He was going to work harder than ever in rehab and come back stronger. He wasn't giving up on basketball. He wasn't giving up on himself.

His eighth-grade season might have ended on the bench, but his journey was far from over.

CHAPTER 4:
TRYOUTS

Months passed, and MVP's knee healed. Through grueling physical therapy and endless hours of training, he pushed himself harder than ever. Every painful stretch, every frustratingly slow drill, every setback fueled his determination. He was going to prove to everyone, especially himself, that he was still MVP.

But his recovery wasn't smooth. The first time he tried sprinting; his knee buckled beneath him. The first time he attempted a jump shot, his landing sent a jolt of pain through his leg. He had to sit out of scrimmages and watch from the sidelines again.

"Take it slow," the trainer reminded him. "Pushing too hard too soon could set you back."

But patience had never been his strong suit. MVP kept trying, pushing through the discomfort, determined to regain his form. But every time he tried to match his old speed, his old moves, his old confidence, something felt off. His knee hesitated; his instincts wavered. He wasn't the same player he had been before.

Still, by the time high school tryouts arrived, he told himself he was ready. He ignored the lingering tightness in his leg and the small voice in his head whispering doubts. This was his moment to reclaim his spot.

He gave it his all, moving across the court with as much speed and agility as he could muster. He nailed his shots, executed plays, and fought to shake off any hesitation. But something was missing. His movements weren't as smooth, his reactions a half-second too slow. He was playing well, but not great.

When the final whistle blew, he took a deep breath. He was sure he'd done enough.

"Great job, gentlemen," the coach announced. "Results from tryouts will be posted tomorrow outside the gym."

That night, MVP barely slept. He replayed the tryout over and over, second-guessing every moment.

The next day, his heart pounded as he scanned the roster. His eyes darted straight to the varsity list to look for his name. Then, his stomach dropped.

"THE FRESHMAN TEAM!?" he read in disbelief. "I made the freshman team?"

This wasn't supposed to happen. He had worked so hard. He was supposed to be on varsity, proving that he had come back stronger. Instead, it felt like he had failed.

"Looks like we'll be playing together again this year, MVP," Roman, a fellow teammate, said.

MVP clenched his jaw. "Call me Micah," he muttered, walking away. He didn't feel like MVP anymore.

CHAPTER 5:
MICAH

Micah was saddened by the results, and his confidence took a massive hit. The moment he saw his name on the freshman roster, something inside him cracked. He had tried. He had fought. He hadn't given up like he'd wanted to many times. But none of that was enough.

He loved basketball, though. So, what could he do? He tried to make the best of his position on the freshman team. At first, he attended every practice, ran drills, and showed up for team meetings. But he wasn't the same. The fire that had once pushed him to stay late after practice and wake up early to train had burned out.

He stopped pushing himself.

He stopped caring.

His shot, once precise and effortless, now felt clumsy.

His speed, once his greatest weapon, had dwindled.

He started skipping extra workouts. What was the point? He wasn't MVP anymore. Maybe he never really had been. Maybe his injury had stolen his chance, or maybe he had just never been as good as he thought.

The time came for his first high school game, but Micah didn't feel the usual excitement. He didn't feel anything. As he pulled on his jersey, it felt heavier than ever. He wasn't sure if he was ready or if he even wanted to play at all.

Before the game, his dad gave him the same reminder he always did. "Remember, son: P.A.S.S. it to me."

"I know, Dad!" Micah snapped, his frustration boiling over.

His father frowned but didn't say anything else.

Micah jogged onto the court, but he might as well have been sleepwalking. Nothing felt right. He missed easy shots. His legs felt slow, and his arms felt heavy. Every pass he made was a half-second too late, every cut he took was just off the mark. The more he tried to get into the rhythm of the game, the more out of sync he felt. It was like his body had forgotten how to play.

The coach pulled him out. Micah walked to the bench; his shoulders slumped. He barely heard the sounds of the game around him.

Roman sat down beside him and nudged his shoulder. "You'll get them next time, MVP," he said.

Micah let out a bitter laugh. "It's Micah, man. Just Micah."

Roman raised his hands in surrender. "Alright, Micah."

The buzzer sounded for halftime, but Micah barely noticed. He stared at the court, his mind churning.

He had tried.

He had fought.

And he had failed.

Maybe he wasn't meant to come back. Maybe this was it.

CHAPTER 6:
P.A.S.S. IT TO ME

In the locker room, the coach was delivering an inspiring halftime speech, but Micah barely heard him. He sat on the bench, staring down at his shoes, feeling the weight of every mistake he'd made. The shots he'd missed. The hesitation in his movements.

His doubts had consumed him.

Roman nudged him. "MVP, when you get open next quarter, pass it to me."

Micah looked up, ready to snap back, but something about the way Roman said it stopped him. Pass it to me. The words echoed in his head, connecting with something familiar. For weeks, he had ignored those words, letting them fade into the background. "P.A.S.S. it to me" was just a silly phrase his father taught him when he was younger and learning how to pray. But now, the words hit him differently and a memory surfaced. Him as a little kid, sitting on his dad's lap, a tiny basketball in his hands as his father taught him how to pray.

"Praise Him for all His goodness."

"Ask for forgiveness."

"Say what's on your heart."

"Sit and wait for God to respond."

Micah exhaled slowly. He had spent so much time trying to force his way back, trying to control every part of his comeback. Maybe this wasn't just about prayer. Maybe this was about trust. Trusting God. Trusting himself, trusting the process, trusting that his story wasn't over just because he was injured.

He closed his eyes. *God, I don't know if I can do this. But I'm giving it to You. Whatever happens, I trust You.*

As he opened his eyes, something inside him shifted. The fear wasn't completely gone, but the weight of it wasn't crushing him anymore. He wasn't alone in this.

The third quarter started, and Micah stepped onto the court with a different energy. He wasn't trying to force anything. He was playing the way he used to. Free. Trusting his instincts. Trusting his team.

The ball found its way to him. Instead of hesitating, instead of second-guessing himself, he reacted. He dribbled, cut through defenders, and when he saw Roman wide open at the three-point line, he didn't think—he passed.

Roman caught it, squared up, and launched the shot. The ball swished cleanly through the net.

Micah grinned.

Play after play, he moved with confidence. He passed when he needed to. He drove when he had the lane. When the final minute came, with the game on the line, he didn't hesitate. He took the shot.

The ball soared through the air, spinning perfectly as it sank into the hoop.

The buzzer blared.

The crowd erupted. His teammates swarmed him.

They had won.

Micah stood in the middle of it all, heart pounding, breathing heavily. For the first time in a long time, he felt like himself again. Maybe even better than before.

He finally understood, he had never been in this alone.

CHAPTER 7:
MVP

"MVP! MVP! MVP!" the crowd chanted.

Micah stood at center court, the echoes of the game still ringing in his ears. His teammates patted his back, the adrenaline still surging through his veins. He had done it. Not just won the game but found himself again.

Roman nudged him. "How are you going to tell them to shout Micah?" he teased.

Micah grinned, shaking his head. "I guess MVP is here to stay."

As they walked off the court, his dad was waiting in the stands, arms crossed, a knowing smile on his face. MVP met his eyes and nodded. "P.A.S.S. it to me," he murmured under his breath, understanding it now in a way he never had before.

Later that night, as he lay in bed, he thought back on everything—the injury, the frustration, the setbacks. He had fought, failed, nearly given up. But through it all, he had learned something more important than just basketball.

He had learned to trust, to grow, to let go of what he couldn't control.

The season was far from over—his journey was just beginning. But for the first time in a long time, he wasn't afraid of what was coming next.

Micah closed his eyes, a small smile playing on his lips.

Whatever happens next, he was ready.